Finally Free

Nijae Ison

Nijae Ison

ISBN: 0-692-13255-4
ISBN-13: 978-0-692-13255-5

Finally Free

DEDICATION

For those of you that never got a chance to tell your story.
If no one remembers you, I will.

CONTENTS

ACKNOWLEDGMENTS

Thank you, Mom and Damon for having patience with me, while I temporarily lost my mind and for encouraging me to do whatever my heart desired. I love you. To all the people that believed in me and pushed me to put myself out there thank you.

Finally Free

Welcome

Finding solace within myself, awareness of my despair, then making the decision to speak about my struggles, were some of the most challenging phases in creating *Finally Free*. Feelings of uncertainty, low self esteem, and not knowing how to look for love within oneself are issues a lot of us deal with silently. The intent of this book is to let people know that they are not alone, and I am willing to be a martyr for the cause. So for those too shy to speak, I will speak my piece within us all.

Finally Free

This title came to me when I had discovered, after years of silence, that I was strong enough to publicly embrace the tender parts of me. I was able to open my heart and my mind, fearless of judgment. I felt secure enough with myself to place pieces of my soul in a book that is open to criticism. I could finally speak without my tongue being anchored by my discomfort and nervousness. On the day that I understood this, I was finally free.

-Nijae Ison

There is no greater agony than bearing an untold story inside you.

-Maya Angelou

Finally Free

FREE.

Sometimes in life you have to fall on your *ass* to, land on your feet.

Power of the womb

I take compliments like free cash these days
No longer apologizing for my beauty
Not when basic men I call my peers
Can comfortably give themselves crowns they don't
Deserve
While being praised for things
I as a woman am "expected" to know
I earned this confidence
I am king, bitch
Until they can feel their uterus contract
And a million daggers landing in their bellies
Until they can feel "their" princes kick them from the
inside
Until they carry the burdens of being a she
Until then as women
We will forever seek reign over the land
Even though they treat us as if
We're supposed to sit quietly in the back seat
Shes give the world life
Carrying the future in our wombs
Even when it stands on our necks
Complaining we're hurting its feet

Love Thy Self

I walk in every room like I own that bitch
Hair flips and pouty lips
Even on my worst day
The sight of me
Makes heads turn
I can make any man thirsty
And I have the sweetest juices to moisten lips
Don't ever think expensive gifts
Can pardon your bullshit
Come correct or don't cum at all
I'd lay in an empty bed for a million nights
Before I let you speak to me like I'm not the one
Like I'm not the prize
If you think otherwise
You can go
I'd rather be alone
Than treated like I deserve anything less than a throne
Anything less than
A diamond encrusted crown placed upon my head
While sitting pretty crushing roses underneath
My pedicured feet
I'm okay with being alone
I alone am my best company
No more being a wife to a boyfriend
Who'd never treat me like a queen
Never marry me

First Off

I used to bite my tongue, not anymore

First off, fuck them and their standards

I only represent myself

If you also have mixed feelings about who you are
and who you should be

Let this be a reminder to you

Make the first move and continue to climb

They'd rather you be down there, miserable and
conforming with them, than in

The clouds making your dreams

Come true

Too Black

The world told me I'm too loud
Too black
Too proud
And I should conform to expressions they considered
appropriate
I chose to be free
Speaking my truth confidently
I am forever indebted to
The men and women that made me it possible for me
To have a voice that has the ability to reach the
masses
I've felt the weight of the world on my shoulders
Pushing me to the ground
Demanding me to beg for its mercy
But I would not give up without a fight
Although at times it has regretfully crossed my mind
It is for them I am still standing
Still strong

You Would Have Thought

They always come to me full of hope
Perceiving my smiles and laughter
As innocence
It's either my age or how I carry myself
That I can trick the right fool
Into believing I'd let him lead me
To the pits of hell
Or if he charmed me enough
I'd tolerate blatant di

Do not ask for permission

Some will give you backhanded compliments
Some don't want you to be happy
The highest paid
The most liked
They would rather you tilt your head hiding your face
So they could be more comfortable in their own skin
Stop asking them for permission
If you had nothing to offer, you would not intimidate
them

Golden

Not long ago I decided I was going to be
Unapologetically me
I would no longer stand behind barriers of shame
I am gold
And I will not apologize if the shine from this gold
Hurts your eyes
I worked too hard learning how to stand on my own
Two feet
I have no time to entertain your
Ideas of who you think I should be
Because you see I am gold
And I will not apologize when my shine blinds you

Still Here

This is bigger than me.

It's much more than just words strung together

This is my truth for the people who share comparable stories. I've felt heartbreak that I thought would consume me. I am still here and so are you.

Murder

You can see the confidence

Dripping off of me

You thought your words could cut deep

Only to be met with the greatest disconnect

I used to love you more than sex

You wanted the feeble version of the woman

Standing in front of you

I murdered her

In cold blood

With a smirk on my face

Self Love

I didn't know how to love what I couldn't see
Even that was hard for me
I will change
I will grow old and age, and the person staring back at
Me
Will not look the same
Learning to love my soul was hard
To love something I couldn't see was once too grand
For me
I'm thankful
I took a leap of faith within me

Wings

I thank him for letting me go
For letting me fly
I think he thought it would kill me
Even I thought I might die
He did not know and neither did I
I would land in the feathers of another
Who helped show me how to mend
My damaged wings
I evolved into the woman
I thought I would never be
Not for either of them
But for me
When the caged bird is finally set free

Finally Free

NUMB

Finally Free

No Idea

His hands grip my hips

Today I fell victim to his advances

Something had switched

This will be the last time we embrace

I have to stop loving him so I can learn to love me

He has no idea so he

Speaks I love you's that will dance on deaf ears

And fall on a ghostly heart

F over R

I have a better understanding of my own cogitation

I think I understand my love of fornication

More than relationships now

I fantasize about his hands inching up my thighs

I can't even imagine having him to myself

So for now I take what he gives me

Ass slaps and sweet texts

No strings attached

What if I told you
All I wanted was a taste of your body
And I didn't want the false idea of love
You were selling
What if I told you
I wanted hard sex
With no strings attached
Would you squint your eyes in confusion
Because I am a woman
And I am only to desire a relationship
Should I keep an empty space
In my bed just for you while you occupy the beds of
Others?
Am I expected to blindly compete with them?
Playing a game where all the participants have
Nothing to gain
But you

Selfish

I planted kisses all over his face

Missing his touch

I loved the idea that I would leave after this and it

Would be perfectly normal that we didn't speak after this

I knew he wanted to know me more

But the way life works it just couldn't work out that way

And that was okay

We couldn't fight over conversations that didn't happen

I didn't care who he slept with besides me

It was okay as long as

When we were together it was all about me

My Idea of Healing

One hand gripped my curls

As his momentum quickened behind me

I challenged him to get buried inside of me

Until my body could no longer ask for more

Sweat the only thing between us

Tequila on my breath

The room was spinning

I wondered how long it would take for him

To get lost inside me

While he caressed my skin

Alone

Let's embark on our expedition

Make me quiver

Time has stopped and

It feels like we're alone in the world

Kisses planted on gasping lips

Strands of my hair

At your fingertips

Ecstasy

The butterflies are back

Hanging out in my stomach

Every time I look at you

They flutter in support

While you stand there naked

My heart is pounding

As if it might explode

I just received my round trip ticket to

Ecstasy

Nervous

Experimenting with this, I'm nervous

Not my first time but my first time with you

We fight to reach the bed

Hurrying to take our clothes off

Then I get the feeling of

Warm lips on my abdomen

He tells me I have the softest skin

Excited and terrified I prepare to pretend

But silk pillowcases muffle my moans

At no time before today

Had I the luxury of feeling waves

Of pleasure so pure

They spread through me from my head to my toes

It's pimp or die

I don't want to be clingy

He'll lose interest

But how can he not

I've already given him all I feel I'm worth

He's touched every inch of me

How could I respectfully ask for

Anything more

Curve

I'm asking questions getting no genuine answers

From you

You know what it feels like

To let someone into you

Then getting no hit ups from you

It's still new

But my walls will forever remember you

In a week or two I will forget about you too

I'll no longer cringe when I see your face pop up on my timeline

Or one of those cool pictures you drew

Till then I'll reminisce over thoughts of you

UNDERSTANDING

Finally Free

If You Must

Chase me if you must

But you could never make me stay

I could never be yours

I'm a slave to my fears

I'd rather be one with the world

Then one with you

Sure anyone would die to be

Treated like a queen

But I know it's surreal

I know it's untrue

I know no matter how much you give

One day I'll pay the price

For a so-called

Beautiful life

To be nothing but your beautiful Wife

The women I know

Hold stretch marks on their skin

Bearing children that only look

Like the men

So hold your ring

I'll keep my youth

My body won't hold the scars

Of the ugly truth

Frogs

I used to fall in love with almost every man

That showed me an inch of consideration

I was always easily convinced

Were they taking the time to know me

Or was the allure of the space between my thighs

Appealing enough?

Yet how would I know authentic "love?"

When the person that was designated to teach me

The devotion of a man broke my heart unjustifiably

Before it had the chance to develop

Can you blame me for always falling for the
Compassionate

Bullshit that flowed from most of their lips?

Kissing every frog wishing this time it'd be a prince

Mr. Charming

He was so effortlessly charming.

It made me want to straddle him naked and rip his eyes out.

This is exactly why I could not trust myself, when under the spell of their soothing tones.

Let them boldly profess their buttery words.

Quickly all was forgiven but this time around, I thought I was different.

Smarter

Once again you're falling

You said it'd be different this time

Loving no one and nothing

So you can leave and feel nothing like them

You have been a prisoner of love before

You were supposed to close your heart

And open your eyes

You were supposed to be able to see when

Men were devils in disguise

For Me

It was like he could sense

Every time I wanted to leave him

He had me melted in his palms

I couldn't deny how much happier I was

He provided me with words of endearment

He loved every curve and stretch mark on my body

It was as if God had made him just for me

Remembering

He told me why he left his ex, and how. It made remember why I never wanted to be in love again. I was terrified I would fall so deeply in love for that same man to one day wake up and decide he didn't love me anymore. I felt my stomach turn as I imagined his departure. The feeling brought chills down my spine. The memories flashed back in my brain over and over again I looked up at him, speechless, with widened eyes. He didn't know that at that very moment I would never let myself love him fully. I would never again allow myself to be so vulnerable.

Finally Free

Stockholm Syndrome

He pushes me I pull him closer

One day I will fall off this cliff

I have not yet learned what happens when you play
with fire

My fingers are not yet sore and blistered

To pull someone close to you when they are unwilling
to be kept, is to stand in front of a hungry animal
asking not to be eaten

You will surely die slowly

And painfully

I was captured

Then freed

The Stockholm syndrome had kicked in because when you hated me you still showed me more love than them

The sex kept me numb; the lack of sent me over

I fell hitting every rock below, I could not love you when I could not feel you

When the last bit of your affection no longer existed my false reality of us

Disappeared too

Words Hurt

I slayed him with my words

They hit him harder than any fist could

He had slithered in my life like he'd done to plenty
before me

Expecting me to succumb to his charm

I learned my lesson

When the hands of the person whom I had thought
loved me

Gripped my throat until I turned blue

Physical or mental I would not

Let anyone abuse my temple

Engrossed

I was engrossed with the impersonation of a man.

So I am now digging up the remains of my

Shattered heart

Bruised as fuck

Scratching at the me I used to be

My idea of love changed for forever

Jagged edges with foggy vision

I started to believe every man was the enemy

Pill Popper

I had a dream

One in which I was in love with him again

During a time when even the concept of him

Disingenuously loving another woman

Made me want to reacquire him as my acquisition

He pushed me hard enough

Fracturing the part of my brain

That conditioned me on

How I was to be treated by a man

I loved him more than I loved myself

A handful of pills were a brighter future

Than being without him

Suddenly

I awoke almost too late

Finally Free

LOSING MYSELF

At seventeen I fell for anyone that showed me love.

Traces

The remnants of you

Are forever stained in the crevices of my brain

With time my memory has blurred

But somehow you stick

Like lint on my favorite sweater

You stick like that last square of polish when there's
no acetone in sight

I can't scrape you off

Spending restless nights

Obsessing over what I can do to wash off the traces of
you

Tug of War

I had already lost the game of tug of war

Only I couldn't differentiate the winner

He refused to make eye contact

As I screamed and tears rolled down my cheeks

I couldn't breathe

I didn't know how to live without him

I look into his eyes and see

A person that did not love me

Loved

No matter how hard you try

I will not take no for an answer

You can't just walk out of my life

It doesn't work like that

I didn't want you here in the first place

You tricked me into being with you

For you to take it all back

Leaving me with less than what I started with

Was your goal to leave me broken?

Without the possibility of ever being fixed

So no matter how many men

Try to repair the wounds you left

I wouldn't ever love them how

I loved you

Changes

I love you

Came rushing out from the back of his mouth

He kissed my lips

A gleeful grin followed

He embraced my body then looked at me

As if I was the most delightful thing nature had made

Specifically for his pleasure

This continued for weeks

Then the kisses began to lessen

And the hugs began to slow

Then one day he said he didn't love me anymore

Never you

He showed you

He showed you more than once who he was and what he could be

But you still choose to ignore

You still choose to be purposely blind to your visions

It was easier to swallow than to feel lesser than

So you held on to that false reality

Did you think you were better than the ones before you?

You might have been, but he would not let go of them for you

Once you turned your no into a yes you were lost forever

He was a horrible teacher

Teaching you to expect more from even the worst of them

Still here you are with watery eyes over another man that makes it

Clear it would never be you

Millionth Time

We bantered slightly with the aroma of sex, pungent in the air. A break came in the conversation I was too nervous to look in his direction. Then at once we turned to each other locked eyes and asked, "Did you miss me?" As if we had practiced this for hours. A smile covered each of our faces. At that moment, it was confirmed. I had fallen in love with the same man, for the millionth time.

Empty

My eyes were puffy and red

He looked at me emotionless

I still loved him

The same man that had bruised my skin

I felt heavy again

I felt the empty space I tried to fill

With him open up again

I choked on the words that were falling

From my mouth

I just wanted us to be together again

I wanted him to pretend to love me again

This prince of darkness tricked me once again

How could you love a man that left bruises on

Your skin

I asked myself again

The Other

I fell in love with the idea of us

He wasn't mine because he came to the rescue

At the perfect time

I had to be selfish

for my heart

I was starting to fall apart

Sometimes I wish I would've ran from the start

but then I wouldn't be the person I am today

He helped me remember my beauty and my worth

After leaving a person that wouldn't put me first

He wouldn't either but it was a start

I learned how to tell two men apart

Hopeless Romantic

I believed every word he said. It was I love you's minus him actually saying it. I told myself in secret. He expressed it in other ways. You can tell by the way a man looks at you right? I'd feel his stares from across the room. It was admiration not lust. He had seen the light that shined off of me when imbeciles ignored.

Each word landed so gracefully on my love struck ears. My defense mechanism kicked in telling me to ignore it. Ignore your feelings of trust and calmed nerves. He will let you slip from his clasp with no intentions of catching you. I was forever in a constant battle.

Story Teller

He told beautiful stories

And I ate them up

Leaving me stuffed

But malnourished

We'd lay in bed

Intertwined

Dreaming of what could be

One day I would have to face the reality of this union

Lie to Me

I loved his deceit

It kept my mind at peace

I was okay with the dishonesty

Back when it was easy for me to let go

Now I'm stuck between yes and no

He caught me slippin

Overanalyzing the picture he painted for me

No motion in his plan

I am stagnant in these waters

Of beginning and end

Love or lust it is for me to choose

Either way I'm pretty sure I'll always lose

How many kisses

I still believed

I was a princess

And one day

I would be treated like a queen

I left hints

Thinking then he would understand

Why he had been graced

With my presence

Praying the sweet ideas

I planted would grow and manifest in the next few weeks

I crossed my fingers and waited

Imagining him being my true king

12

My relationship with men has almost always been
tumultuous.

I Apologize

So many women who surrounded me shared similar stories

Yet I didn't hear them until I had my own

By then it was too late

I thought I was the only one

That had to sit across a table

Eating breakfast with a man I hated

The knife was always so close

At times I thought of holding it to his throat

Or perhaps my own

Hoping God would do me a favor and give me a
second chance

At life

If I couldn't save you I'm sorry

But I pray I give you the strength to tell somebody

On TV

I was allotted a week off from my high school because I had lost a parent.

I missed only two days.

I couldn't stay home.

I didn't trust myself alone with my thoughts.

I couldn't tell anyone until the next week.

How could I tell half the story?

How do you explain to your friends,

You were hurting for years and refused to tell anyone

But when you did, he took the easy way out leaving you to clean up the mess.

I just wanted to be happy and carefree like the girls on TV.

Basic

I used to feel basic as fuck

For thinking I could help someone

Telling someone it's okay to speak

I wish I could be like some and

Ignore my discomfort

And pretend I always had my shit together

But I want to help

Someone who at one point and

sometimes still feels disgusted in their own skin

Around any and all men

Silence

His death angered me

I didn't get the chance to tell him how I felt

Preparing myself to testify

Looking him in his eyes as I recounted all the things he did to me

He was evil

The person that makes up half of me

I'd cry when he yelled at me

Screaming at me while his gold tooth flashing in my face

He made me feel small

Unimportant

Stupid

As an adult, I now understand that he had to make me feel weak so that I wouldn't speak

Finally Free

The War

To cover your skin with the hottest water you could take washing him off you.

To weep quietly in that same shower so your sounds would not wake the others sleeping.

To watch the world you thought you knew be shattered before your eyes.

To forever waking up from your deepest slumber at the sound of an opening door.

To have secretly vowed to take your shame to the grave.

To hold your silence for four years before someone else spoke the same secret as you.

To finally speak having your life's most embarrassing
moments written out and recounted back to you by
strangers.

To watch your aunt wag her finger blaming you for
the death of her brother at his funeral, who committed
suicide days earlier.

To be angered and confused that you were saddened
by your father's death crying for a man that forever
changed your perception of people forever.

To speak my secrets candidly to anyone that would
listen and almost always getting a similar story back.

To help others who have been or will be silenced by
shame, fear, or embarrassment by telling my story.

Is me being a survivor of a war I never signed up for.

FREEDOM

For years I danced with the devil, a battle of being my best me or lying in bed indefinitely. Thoughts of suicide had crossed my mind frequently. I could no longer recognize who I was. I had branded myself with the title of "contaminated." *Whom could I turn to without outing myself?* I was changing. I was getting colder. I planned on puncturing his lungs while he slept.

I was twelve with the weight of my secrets slowly crushing my conscience. I was twelve years old when the molestation started, at the hands of my own father. If I didn't tell her, my mother wouldn't know her oldest child was damaged. She wouldn't go to jail, for murdering him like I thought she would. I asked God more than once, "Why me?" Why did he have to pick this life, this family for me? Then a day came and I made the decision to just deal with it. If no one knew, then it was as if it never happened. I would never be embarrassed. I would never be labeled a victim. I would never have to speak to the police. I would never have to watch my mother cry because she felt she failed me. My plan was to wait until I was eighteen, change my name, move away and never speak to anyone again. I was never going to tell a soul. Four years later, someone close to me had spoken before I turned eighteen.

I was sixteen when my mother came into my room and told me my father had been arrested, for sexually assaulting young girls. I knew from that day on my life would never be the same. I knew she was now questioning every weekend I'd ever spent with him.

I still didn't have it in my heart to tell her the truth. She asked me more than once. I looked her in the eyes with the blankest expression; I could conjure and said, "No, mom he's never did anything to me, anything else?" I pretended to be annoyed, praying she'd leave me alone with my thoughts. She did. I called my best friend at the time. When I told her the news, she asked me if I believed the accusations being brought against him. I matter-of-factly said, "I know." It took a little while before she understood.

Strangely enough I didn't cry when she got sad for me. It didn't feel real; it was as if time had stopped. I was emotionless that night. I couldn't stop tears in my early morning history class. My vision was blurred. My hands were shaking.

It had been a year since the last incident. I thought it was over, but it had only begun. It stopped for me and started with someone else. She had the courage I didn't, to tell someone. I thought it was only happening to me. I could've saved her, she would've never had to suffer like I did, my mind raced. I asked to be excused and left class early. I went to speak to my cross-country coach.

She was the second person I told. She held me and together we cried. When she told my mom, I felt the weight lift off my shoulders. I was blessed to have a family and friends that supported me. In a week's time, I learned almost all the women I knew and loved knew what it felt like to have their bodies violated. I listened to old stories, new to my ears, flow from the lips of my many heroes.

All I could think was, why were we having these conversations after I had already suffered so much? Why were these stories told in secrecy, until now? I had always been told to beware, but I never knew they, too, had felt my pain. A few months later, on a day he was supposed to appear in court, my father killed himself. I was relieved that my secret was out, and he could no longer harm anyone else, but it didn't bring me the closure I had expected.

While looking at him in his casket, he was no longer scary to me. His face looked just like mine. As I listened to his mother cry, mourning the death of her youngest child, I cried. too. In one moment, I lost my greatest villain, and the person that contributed to making half of me. Two months after his death, I turned seventeen. My birthday fell on Father's Day. Talk about irony. I was pissed. For years, I went through cycles of dating men that were both mentally and physically abusive. I loved them with no regard for my own happiness and wellbeing.

It took me years to understand the correlation between the men I loved and slept with and my relationship with my father. I thought I could help them, when I couldn't help the person looking back at me in the mirror. Through these men, I was looking for love that I could only give myself. I'm still recovering from the damage. But I gave myself a chance to live another day and I'm thankful for having made that choice.

I'm not embarrassed anymore. I volunteer my story whenever the opportunity presents itself, and I always get stories back. Most had not unveiled their darkest secrets to anyone before speaking to me. My goal is to make these conversations no longer taboo.

This is my truth.

It has only made me stronger.

I hope one day we all, can finally be free.

We know the pain is real,
but you can't heal what you never reveal.

- Sean Carter

Finally Free

ABOUT THE AUTHOR

Nijae is an up and coming artist. She is from both flushing New York and North Bergen New Jersey. Currently residing in New York. A mother to her only son hunter, she brings you a rawness seldom seen. Letting you into her thoughts. Showing you life through her eyes. Where you can either feel like you're walking down a runway or walking through muddy trenches. She wants to show the world, it's okay to be comfortable in your own skin. It's okay, to tell those stories that make you uncomfortable. It's okay to let yourself free. This is just the beginning of the story.